THE WEAVING THREADS OF INDIA

THE UNEXPLORED SIGNIFICANCE OF MUSLIMS

ADIL FIROZ KHAN

Made with ♥ on the Notion Press Platform
www.notionpress.com

To Firoz Khan, my beloved father, who has always been a source of encouragement and inspiration in my life. Your unwavering support and belief in my abilities have helped me to pursue my passions and follow my dreams. This book is dedicated to you, with deep gratitude and love, for all the sacrifices you have made and for being a constant source of strength and guidance.

Contents

Preface

India's cultural tapestry is a rich and vibrant mosaic of diverse traditions, religions, and customs. As a land of many cultures, India has always been a melting pot of ideas and a hub of intellectual and artistic activity. Yet, for many years, the contributions of one of India's most significant communities - the Muslims - have been overlooked or misrepresented in historical accounts. This book, "The Weaving Threads of India: The Unexplored Significance of Muslims," seeks to address this gap, by exploring the vital role that Muslims have played in shaping India's history, culture, and society.

As a writer and researcher, I have always been fascinated by India's cultural diversity and religious plurality. Through my travels and research, I have gained a unique perspective on the contributions made by the Muslim community to India's rich and complex cultural tapestry. It is my hope that this book will shed light on these contributions and help to promote greater understanding and appreciation of the many threads that make up the cultural fabric of India.

The book is organized into several chapters, each focusing on a different aspect of the Muslim community's contributions to Indian society. Through an exploration of art, music, literature, and society, readers will gain a deeper appreciation for the role played by Muslims in shaping India's cultural landscape. Additionally, this book aims to provide a balanced and nuanced understanding of the challenges and opportunities faced by the Muslim community in India today.

Ultimately, "The Weaving Threads of India" is a celebration of diversity, resilience, and vitality. It is a tribute to the Muslim community's rich and multifaceted contributions to India, and an invitation to explore the many threads that make up the cultural tapestry of this fascinating and complex country.

Acknowledgements

I would like to express my heartfelt gratitude to my family, especially my parents, Noorjahan Khan and Firoz Khan, and my aunt, Afsana Khan, for their unwavering love and support throughout this journey. Their encouragement and belief in me have been the driving force behind this book, and I could not have completed it without their constant support.

To my parents, I am forever grateful for your unconditional love and support. Your guidance and encouragement have been a constant source of inspiration, and I am blessed to have you as my parents.

To my aunt Afsana Khan, thank you for always being there for me, no matter what. Your belief in my abilities and unwavering support have been a source of strength and inspiration.

To my siblings Ahmed & Aafia, thank you for always being my support system. Your love for me have been instrumental in completing this book.

I also extend my heartfelt thanks to my extended family members who have been a constant source of support and encouragement. Your belief in me and your unwavering support have been instrumental in completing this book.

To my family, who has always been my rock, I dedicate this book. Your love and support have been the bedrock of my life, and I am forever grateful.

Prologue

India has a rich and diverse history, one that is often overlooked or misrepresented. As a Muslim in India, I have always felt a deep connection to the country and its past. Growing up, I often heard stories of the Mughal Empire and the contributions that Muslims made to India's cultural heritage. However, I also realized that many of these stories were distorted or omitted altogether from mainstream narratives.

As I delved deeper into India's history, I began to uncover a wealth of untold stories, of Muslim leaders, scholars, poets, and artists who left an indelible mark on the country's cultural and political landscape. Their contributions were not limited to just the past but continue to shape India's present and future.

Through this book, I hope to shine a light on the important role that Muslims have played in India's history and to challenge the stereotypes and misconceptions that have plagued the community for far too long. It is a tribute to the many Muslims who have left an indelible mark on the country and a call to all Indians to embrace the diversity and richness of their shared heritage.

ONE
INTRODUCTION

Muslims have been an integral part of India's cultural and political fabric for over a thousand years. From the Mughal Empire to the modern-day, the community has made significant contributions to the country's literature, art, architecture, politics, and more. Despite this, the community often faces discrimination and marginalization, with their contributions to Indian history and culture frequently overlooked or dismissed.

In this book, we seek to showcase the importance of Muslims in India and their contributions to the country's history and culture. We delve deep into the rich and diverse history of the Muslim community in India, exploring their achievements, their struggles, and their contributions to the country's cultural heritage.

Through this book, we hope to challenge the stereotypes and misconceptions that have plagued the Muslim community and provide a comprehensive and engaging account of their place in India's history. We aim to create an inclusive narrative that celebrates the diversity and richness of India's cultural and political heritage and encourages all Indians to embrace and appreciate the contributions of Muslims to their shared history.

TWO

The Arrival of Islam in India

THREE

The Struggle for Independence and Partition

The struggle for India's independence from the British Raj was a significant turning point in the country's history. Muslims played a vital role in the independence movement, and their contributions were instrumental in securing India's freedom from British rule. However, the quest for independence was not without challenges and obstacles.

The early 20th century saw the rise of the Indian National Congress, a political party that aimed to secure India's independence from British rule. The party included several prominent Muslim leaders, such as Muhammad Ali Jinnah and Abul Kalam Azad. These leaders played an essential role in the struggle for independence and were instrumental in shaping India's political landscape.

However, the Indian National Congress's stance towards Muslims was not always welcoming. The Congress often ignored the demands of the Muslim community, leading to growing resentment among the Muslim population. This growing discontent among Muslims led to the formation of the All India Muslim League in

1906, a political party that aimed to represent the interests of the Muslim community.

The Muslim League played a crucial role in the struggle for independence and demanded a separate Muslim homeland, which eventually led to the creation of Pakistan in 1947. The demand for Pakistan was rooted in the idea of a separate Muslim identity, and the League argued that Muslims could not live in a Hindu-dominated India.

The League's demand for Pakistan met with fierce resistance from the Congress, and tensions between the two parties escalated in the years leading up to independence. The Quit India movement, launched by the Congress in 1942, was a significant turning point in the struggle for independence, with both the Congress and the League coming together to demand the end of British rule in India.

The partition of India in 1947 was a traumatic event in the country's history and had a profound impact on the social, cultural, and political fabric of the country. The partition led to the mass migration of millions of people, with Hindus and Sikhs leaving Pakistan and Muslims leaving India. The violence and bloodshed that followed the partition left a lasting scar on the psyche of the Indian people.

Despite the challenges and obstacles faced by Muslims in the struggle for independence, their contributions to the cause of India's freedom were significant. Muslims such as Maulana Abul Kalam Azad and Khan Abdul Ghaffar Khan played a crucial role in the independence movement, and their contributions were vital in shaping India's political and social landscape.

Through their struggles and sacrifices, the Muslim community played a critical role in securing India's freedom from British rule. The legacy of these Muslim leaders and their contributions to the independence movement continues to inspire generations of Indians, reminding them of the power of unity and the importance of working towards a common goal.

FOUR

CHALLENGES AND OPPORTUNITIES IN THE POST-INDEPENDENCE ERA

The post-independence era in India was marked by significant challenges and opportunities. While India had achieved freedom from British rule, the country faced immense challenges in rebuilding itself and shaping its future. Muslims in particular faced several challenges and opportunities in the post-independence era, as they struggled to find their place in a new, independent India.

One of the significant challenges faced by Muslims was the question of their identity. With the partition of India, the Muslim community had gained a separate homeland in Pakistan, but those who chose to remain in India had to reconcile themselves to the idea of living in a predominantly Hindu nation. This struggle for identity and acceptance would define the Muslim community's place in post-independence India.

Another significant challenge faced by the Muslim community was their representation in government and public life. While several Muslim leaders played a crucial role in the struggle for independence, the post-independence era saw a decline in their influence and power. This decline was largely due to the rise of the Indian National Congress and the sidelining of the Muslim League.

The post-independence era also presented several opportunities for Muslims in India. The Indian constitution, for example, guaranteed religious freedom and provided for affirmative action for minority communities. This paved the way for the emergence of several prominent Muslim leaders in politics and public life, such as Zakir Hussain and Fakhruddin Ali Ahmed.

The Green Revolution, a significant agricultural movement that aimed to increase crop yields and improve food security, also presented several opportunities for Muslims. The movement saw the introduction of high-yielding crops, improved irrigation techniques, and the mechanization of agriculture, which led to an increase in employment opportunities for farmers, including Muslim farmers.

However, despite the opportunities presented by the post-independence era, the Muslim community continued to face significant challenges in India. Communal tensions and violence remained a persistent issue, with several incidents of religious violence erupting in various parts of the country. The Babri Masjid demolition in 1992 and the Gujarat riots in 2002 were some of the most significant instances of communal violence in recent Indian history.

The post-independence era in India was characterized by several challenges and opportunities, and the Muslim community faced both. The struggle for identity and representation in government and public life, as well as communal violence, remained significant challenges for the Muslim community. At the same time, affirmative action, the Green Revolution, and the emergence of prominent Muslim leaders presented several opportunities for the community. The Muslim community's story in post-independence India is one of resilience and perseverance in the face of adversity, and it continues to shape the country's social, cultural, and political landscape to this day.

FIVE

CELEBRATING MUSLIM CULTURE AND DIVERSITY

India is a land of diversity, with many different religions, cultures, and traditions coexisting side by side. One of the most vibrant and influential cultures in India is the Muslim culture, which has contributed greatly to the richness of the country. In this chapter, we will explore the many aspects of Muslim culture and how it is celebrated in India.

From music and dance to cuisine and art, Muslim culture has left an indelible mark on India. Some of the most famous forms of music in India, such as qawwali and ghazals, are closely associated with the Muslim community. These musical genres are an expression of the devotion and spirituality of the Muslim faith, and they are celebrated by people of all faiths in India.

Similarly, the traditional dance forms of India, such as Kathak and Bharatanatyam, have also been influenced by Muslim culture. The famous Kathak dancer, Birju Maharaj, is a Muslim and has played a major role in popularizing this dance form across the world.

Muslim cuisine is also an important part of India's food culture. The Mughal Empire, which ruled India for more than two centuries, introduced a range of delicacies, including biryani, kebabs, and nihari, which are enjoyed by people of all faiths in India today. The sweet dishes of the Muslim community, such as sheer khurma and phirni, are also very popular.

Muslim culture has also contributed significantly to India's art and architecture. The Mughal era was known for its grand monuments, such as the Taj Mahal and the Red Fort, which are among India's most iconic structures. The intricate designs and decorations of these buildings reflect the artistic brilliance of the Muslim community.

Despite the many contributions of the Muslim community to India, there have been challenges as well. The rise of communal tensions in recent years has led to instances of violence and discrimination against Muslims. However, there have also been efforts to celebrate the diversity and richness of India's Muslim culture.

In conclusion, Muslim culture is an integral part of India's cultural tapestry, and it has contributed significantly to the country's diversity and richness. By celebrating this culture and promoting mutual respect and understanding, we can build a more harmonious and inclusive society.

SIX

CONCLUSION

The story of Muslim heritage in India is a rich and complex one, woven together from many different threads of history, culture, and identity. As we have seen in this book, Muslims have made countless contributions to India's development and prosperity, and have left an indelible mark on the country's cultural and social fabric.

At the same time, the Muslim community has also faced many challenges and struggles, from the arrival of Islam to the challenges of post-independence India. But through it all, Muslims in India have persevered, carving out a place for themselves and their culture in this diverse and vibrant nation.

As we move forward into the future, it is important to remember the lessons of the past, and to build a more inclusive and equitable society that values and respects the contributions of all communities, including Muslims. Only by weaving together the many threads of our diverse heritage can we create a tapestry that truly reflects the richness and depth of Indian culture.

Through this book, I hope to have sparked a deeper appreciation for the Muslim legacy in India, and to inspire readers to continue exploring the many stories and threads that make up our shared heritage.

Sources, Further Reading, And Acknowledgments

Bibliography:

Ali, M. M. (2003). Muslims in India: The Growth and Influence of Islam in the Nations of Asia and Central Asia. New York, NY: Oxford University Press.

Jalal, A. (2016). Partisans of Allah: Jihad in South Asia. Cambridge, MA: Harvard University Press.

Hasan, Z. (2014). Legacy of a Divided Nation: India's Muslims Since Independence. New York, NY: Oxford University Press.

Ahmed, I. (2019). India: A New History. New York, NY: Random House.

Further Reading:

Naqvi, S. H. A. (2017). Islam in India: Its Historical, Socio-Cultural and Political Aspects. New Delhi, India: Sterling Publishers Pvt. Ltd.

Basu, A. (2018). Muslims in India: A Political History. Princeton, NJ: Princeton University Press.

Engineer, A. A. (2016). The Muslim Question in India: Political History, Theology, and Law. New Delhi, India: Three Essays Collective.

Acknowledgments:

I would like to express my heartfelt gratitude to my family, who have always been my constant source of support and encouragement. I would also like to thank my aunt, Afsana Khan, for her invaluable insights and feedback throughout the writing process.

I am indebted to the scholars and researchers whose work has informed and inspired this book, as well as to the many individuals and communities who have shared their stories and experiences with me over the years.

Finally, I would like to thank the readers for their time and interest in this book. It is my sincere hope that it will help to deepen our understanding and appreciation of the rich and diverse tapestry of Indian culture, and to inspire us to build a more inclusive and equitable society for all.

9 798889 860822

Printed by Libri Plureos GmbH in Hamburg,
Germany